HOW

Climbing: Knots

Nate Fitch and Ron Funderburke

GUILFORD, CONNECTICUT
HELENA, MONTANA

FALCONGUIDES®

An imprint of Rowman & Littlefield

Falcon, FalconGuides, Outfit Your Mind, and How to Climb are
registered trademarks of Rowman & Littlefield.

Distributed by NATIONAL BOOK NETWORK

British Library Cataloguing in Publication Information available

Library of Congress Cataloging-in-Publication Data

Fitch, Nate.
  Climbing: knots / Nate Fitch and Ron Funderburke.
    pages cm
  ISBN 978-1-4930-0981-7 (pbk.) — ISBN 978-1-4930-1506-1
(ebook) 1. Climbing knots. I. Funderburke, Ron. II. Title.
  GV200.19.K56F58 2015
  796.522—dc23

                                        2015021786

∞™ The paper used in this publication meets the minimum
requirements of American National Standard for Information Sci-
ences—Permanence of Paper for Printed Library Materials, ANSI/
NISO Z39.48-1992.

Warning: Climbing is a dangerous sport. You can be seriously injured or die. Read the following before you use this book.
This is an instruction book about rock climbing, a sport that is inherently dangerous. **Do not depend solely on information from this book for your personal safety. Your climbing safety depends on your own judgment based on competent instruction, experience, and a realistic assessment of your climbing ability.**

The training advice given in this book is based on the author's opinions. Consult your physician before engaging in any part of the training program described by the author.

There are no warranties, either expressed or implied, that this instruction book contains accurate and reliable information. There are no warranties as to fitness for a particular purpose or that this book is merchantable. Your use of this book indicates your assumption of the risk of death or serious injury as a result of climbing's risks and is an acknowledgment of your own sole responsibility for your safety in climbing or in training for climbing.

Rowman & Littlefield and the author assume no liability for accidents happening to, or injuries sustained by, readers who engage in the activities described in this book.

Contents

Introduction

The rope is one of the most expressive and indicative instruments in rock climbing. Much like a climber's body, the behavior, management, and usage of a climbing rope directly reflect the values, efficiency, security, knowledge, and effectiveness of the climbing team. When the rope is deployed skillfully, intentionally, and thoughtfully, the climbing team probably has a commensurate level of skill, intention, and forethought. When the rope is deployed incorrectly, arbitrarily, or lazily, the climbing team probably does not have an appropriate skill level to safely participate in the sport. Perhaps the climbing team simply defaults to patterns and practices that others have demonstrated, without a careful consideration or analysis. Perhaps the climbing team does not appreciate how or why the details really do make a difference when they pertain to staying safe and having fun.

More so than any other tool in the climber's repertoire, the rope is the tool that should be thoroughly understood and deployed in a way that makes a gesture to all other climbers and users: this rope says who I am, how I am doing, and how much I know.

The goal of this text is to deepen a climber's understanding of the use of the climbing rope. Beginners may find this text helpful because the usage of the rope can be learned and practiced. When learning to tie knots and hitches, it is important to practice in a safe learning environment, like a ground school. It's also important to learn to tie knots and hitches with both hands, from different perspectives, and in adverse conditions. Also, the use of online animated resources

With the rope neatly managed, knots and hitches used appropriately, this climbing team is prepared to tackle a complex objective.

can be excellent tools for learning to tie knots and hitches, learning to manage rope, or learning new contexts for ropework.

Intermediate climbers may discover why their mentors and instructors tend to default to the use of certain tools and techniques. There are many options when using a climbing rope, so it is important to

Poor ropework is a warning sign. This climbing team might not be ready for an objective of this magnitude.

understand why some knots predominate while others are forgotten. Most importantly, the use of a particular rope technique has no real merit if there are better alternatives. Intermediate climbers can often benefit from considering more choices, and understanding why a certain technique was selected in the first place, why it is so resilient.

Lastly, more experienced climbers may also benefit from a retreatment of their rope practices. Sometimes, as climbers' understanding of knots and hitches deepens, they become archivists of techniques that don't have any real merit. Experienced climbers often use obscure techniques simply because they are novel, which is a problem when novelty usurps efficiency or the responsibility of being a good mentor to new climbers.

Ultimately, climbers need to remember that the climbing rope is a tool we use to keep each other safe, but it is also a piece of folk art. If the rope is used entirely as a piece of folk art, it can still teach us quite a bit about the culture of climbing, but it probably won't be the most efficient, adaptable, or effective tool. However, if the rope is regarded entirely as a tool, then climbers will also lose touch with the craft, lore, and heritage that has proven to keep all climbers safe, through generations of trial and error. A climbing team is more likely to strike an appropriate balance between artistry and functionality when everyone understands

- the history of a given knot or rope technique,
- the inherent efficiency of tying it and untying it after use,
- how the technique affects the rope's natural strength, and
- the reliability of a knot or rope technique.

When a climbing team understands these basic criteria and uses them to evaluate all rope techniques, certain applications become obvious in certain contexts.

Each section of this text is designed to prepare climbers to solve problems when they are most relevant to their experience. In the beginning, under appropriate mentorship, climbers may not need to know anything more than how to tie in. But soon, they will want to learn to belay and differentiate attachment techniques from each other. As climbers begin to set up topropes and learn to lead climb, anchoring is a routine task. Finally, when climbers begin to look forward to multipitch climbing, improvised self-rescue, or mountaineering, the care and application of the rope will be imperative. All climbers have to start somewhere, and there is something in this text for every climber, wherever climbing takes him/her.

There are also some implicit assumptions throughout this text. First, the writers assume that this text will serve as a complementary resource to an appropriate skills progression. This text is designed to work hand in hand with professional climbing instruction or the dissemination of information from an informal mentor to his/her student. This text is not designed to serve as a substitute for methodical instruction. Also, this text is most effective when read in conjunction with the other books in this series: *From Gym to Rock*, *Protection*, *From Rock to Sport*, and *From Sport to Trad*.

The Rope

Like anything anyone chooses to study carefully, the climbing rope can be studied beyond all value and practical import. All of the rope's contortions, including all knots and hitches, the rope's chemistry and physical attributes, its history and its symbolic value, involve disciplines of science and history that predate rock climbing. An archeologist, for example, can tell us when humans first began to spin fibers into cords, and an anthropologist can tell us why they did it. A chemist, a physicist, and a product engineer can elucidate the way hemp rope molecules interact with heat, dynamic loads, and UV light; they might further contrast that behavior with any number of polyamide, polyethylene, or other synthetic rope materials. Furthermore, even with this level of academic rigor, all climbers have their own experiences and informal tests that confirm, contradict, and complicate the subject. Sometimes scientific and anecdotal expectations coincide; sometimes they do not.

What information do climbers need to know, and what can they leave for the scientists? And how do we communicate all those criteria to each other in a language everyone, scientific or otherwise, can understand? In this chapter we will try to consolidate the way we talk about ropes and ropework. We will draw a climber's attention to the physical properties and behavior of kernmantle ropes and nylon slings with an emphasis on practical use.

Ropes

A modern climbing rope is much different than its predecessors, and it is much different than any other kind of rope available for purchase. A climbing rope almost always is made of nylon and it almost always has a kernmantle construction. We don't have to be industrial engineers to understand why this material and construction are attractive to manufacturers. Nylon is a cheaper material than many other options. It is a versatile material and can easily be used to create small diameter ropes, large diameter ropes, dynamic ropes, and static ropes. The kernmantle construction combines the historical advantages of a twisted rope (in the core) with the braided rope (on the sheath). As a result, nylon can be used to create a product that suits all the applications rock climbers devise for it, in hundreds of colors and patterns.

We don't have to be chemists to understand all the foibles of nylon ropes. Nylon's manufactured strength can be greatly decreased by heat, mildew, mold, chemical contamination, and UV light. Chemists might find more precise ways to describe how much the manufactured strength can be decreased by what temperatures, types and quantity of mold and mildew, and frequency and duration of UV light. But that is not always the most helpful information for rock climbers.

In typical use, we cannot create enough heat through friction to melt our ropes, and we can avoid all other contaminants simply by thinking of the rope as a precious and vital member of our team. We clean it when it's dirty. We dry it when it's wet. We retire it when it's too old and tired to continue climbing, and we keep it away from all the things that could be harmful to it.

Also, we don't have to be surgeons to understand that sharp edges and abrasive surfaces do enormous damage to a climbing rope. While certain knots and hitches can help mitigate these hazards to a climbing rope, it is important to use best practices with anchoring, lead climbing, or toproping to avoid severing nylon ropes.

In this text five different kinds of nylon tools will be described: climbing ropes, static anchoring ropes, cordellette, accessory cord loops, and nylon slings. They each have noteworthy differences in intended application, diameter, length, and elongation.

Remember, the elongation of a rope or cord is one of the most important things for a user to understand, and this principle is the most common basis of the designation of a static or dynamic rope. Elongation generally is measured by how a rope stretches, but that of course depends on how much mass is used to stretch the rope and how the stretching happens.

Rope care is NOT complicated. Treat the rope like a good friend.

- Keep it dry.

- Keep it away from hot things.

- Keep it away from any chemicals you would not want a child to drink.

- Store it in a safe, shaded, dry place.

- Keep it away from sharp or abrasive things.

- Retire it when it is too old or worn out.

- Clean it when it gets dirty.

It should suffice to say that ropes designed for single-strand applications in a climbing system can have enormous elongation, up to 40 percent. That is a good thing, especially for lead climbers. But ropes designated for other purposes, like anchoring, should have very low elongation.

The Climbing Rope

When purchasing a climbing rope, there are dozens of specifications, performance attributes, and styles to choose from. Some climbing ropes are designed to be used in pairs, so they have small diameters and their elongation is based on the two ropes being used in a coordinated fashion. This text, however, will focus the use of a UIAA CE-approved single climbing rope. If a rope is designed for a single-strand application in a climbing system, for belaying any human body weight (even the smallest humans), it not only will have a larger diameter, it also will be clearly labeled for that purpose with ①. Single ropes range from 8.5mm to 11mm in diameter, and they are tested to ensure that a falling climber cannot elongate the rope more than 40 percent of its length or generate an impact force of more than 12kN. Climbers generically refer to the climbing rope as a dynamic rope, even though all

A single climbing rope is clearly indicated by the ①.

nylon ropes have dynamic properties. Climbing ropes generally are sold in manufactured lengths of 60 or 70m. A dry treatment and a clearly defined middle marker are usually well worth the added costs.

Dry treatments can vary in effectiveness and type, but any dry treatment can increase the durability of a rope. Essentially a dry treatment is a chemical coating that sheds water from the rope's sheath. The coating wears off in time, but the initial uses of the rope benefit from this extra layer.

An Anchoring Rope

A second, shorter anchoring rope can be a great tool for toproping anchors; in this application a static rope is appropriate. All rope manufacturers sell these kinds of rope. An anchoring rope should be tough

A static anchoring rope has emerged as the predominant anchoring tool for setting up toprope anchors in a single pitch setting. AMGA Certified Single Pitch Instructors become proficient in the use of this tool.

and durable because it will be used to tie off sharp boulders and trees, and it will usually run over the cliff's edge. A 35m length of 10mm to 11mm nylon rope with less than 5 percent elongation for climbing-related loads would be ideal. These kinds of ropes generally have tensile strength of over 5,000 pounds.

Cordellette

This text also will describe smaller diameter cords and cordellette for use in anchoring systems. A 7mm nylon cord of 5 to 6m length will be more than adequate. Remember, one of the easiest ways to decrease the elongation of a rope system is to double (or triple) the amount of rope. If one strand of 7mm cord, for example, has a manufactured elongation of 9 percent

Cordellettes are helpful tools for constructing anchors when the components are not very far away from one another.

when applied to a 300-pound load, three strands of
that material might conceivably have an elongation of
3 percent. When using ropes and knots for anchoring,
these kinds of maneuvers are used to create an anchor
that minimizes stretching.

Accessory Cord Loops

This text also will describe the use of 5mm or 6mm
nylon accessory cord loops. These are small loops of
nylon used to tie the Prusik and autoblock friction
hitches. An accessory cord loop is never used as a critical
link in any climbing, rappelling, or self-rescue system. So
a loop with a smaller diameter is tolerable because the
relative size of the accessory cord loop and the climbing
rope results in a more effective friction hitch. A friction
hitch or other connection with accessory cord loops
should not be the sole connection to a climbing system.

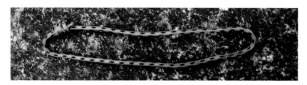

*Even though accessory cord loops are only 5mm nylon,
they are never used as critical links, and the smaller
diameter helps them "grab" larger diameter ropes.
Don't put your friends in a "PICL" (Prusik Is Critical
Link).*

Slings

Unfortunately, ropes and cords can't do everything
climbers need them to do. In particular, climbers need
smaller loops of nylon to create quick attachments

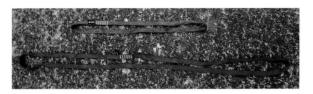

Sewn slings are great tools for attaching two objects to one another, anchoring, or creating a tether. Their versatility makes them superior to other personal anchoring systems.

between objects and carabiners. Lead climbers use slings to secure traditional placements or straighten out a rope line. A short sewn sling between two carabiners is now known as a quickdraw, one of the most iconic tools in sport climbing. Some slings are manufactured, with sewn and professionally rated bar tacks. Some slings are assembled by hand, using 1-inch tubular webbing and water knots. In either case, slings are not designed for climbing in the same way as a climbing rope. They are designed to connect two objects within a system, like connecting a tree (or any other component) to a carabiner, connecting two carabiners to each other, or connecting a climber to an anchor when the rope is not available.

Rope Talk

Learning to tie knots and hitches is easier if we learn how to talk about the rope. Grabbing any segment of the rope, a rope handler should be able to immediately discern his/her proximity to the rope ends.

Ends. Because we will always be using a section of rope in rock climbing, every section has two ends.

Middle. The point of the rope that is equidistant from the ends is, naturally, the middle.

All climbing ropes have two working ends and a middle. The middle marks of these ropes are clearly indicated by a pattern change in the sheath or the black marks on it.

Working End

Grasping a section of the rope designates a standing end and a working end.

Standing end and **working end.** Grasping any section of the rope, there is usually a rope end that will be maneuvered, while the other end of the rope remains stationary. The moving end is called the working end. The stationary end is called the standing end.

Bight. Making any two segments of rope touch each other is called a bight. If the two touching strands are held together, the standing and working ends of

Bight. There is a tongue on one side of the bight and rope ends on the other.

the rope look unique. The working end usually looks like a tongue, and the standing end usually has the rope ends along its length.

Loop. Taking any segment of a rope and twisting it, so that the standing end and the working end cross each other, making a circle, is called a loop. It is important to know that loops have a directional quality. A loop can be made by twisting a segment of the rope in either direction.

Loops have a rotational aspect, an important thing to remember when tying knots such as a bowline.

Guide's Insight

Having taught climbing knots and hitches for a handful of climbing schools, climbing gyms, experiential education programs, and instructor training programs, it has always been intriguing to me that so many climbers learn to tie knots and hitches without the use of any sort of plain language. I have seen climbing instructors give elaborate explanations of how to tie a given knot, using all manner of circumspect analogies, acronyms, and counting games. The irony is that while so many climbers learned to tie knots this way, we never really learned to talk about ropes.

In my own instruction, I first explain the construction of a knot or hitch using plain and simple language, such as, "A figure 8 knot is tied by circumnavigating a tail of rope around a loop one time, before passing the tail through the loop." When this description is accompanied by a visual demonstration to orient the loop and the direction of the tail's travel, most of my students learn to tie the figure 8 knot without my having to resort to invocations of John Travolta, strangled pop singers, or eye-gouged aliens. You'd be amazed at how effective a simple demonstration and some plain language can be.—RF

Knot. All knots require a tail or bight of rope to pass through a loop. If a tail or bight passes through a loop at any point, a knot will be the result.

Hitch. Hitches involve contortions of the rope that require a secondary object, like a carabiner, to hold the hitch in place. If that object were to disappear suddenly, the hitch would unravel.

Bend. Bends are the family of knots used to join two rope ends to each other. Some bends historically were differentiated from knots because removing one rope or the other would unravel the bend. But some joining knots would remain partially intact if one rope or the other were removed. These distinctions are virtually irrelevant to a rock climber. *Bend* and *joining knot* can be used interchangeably to signify a gesture of the rope that joins two rope ends.

After reading this text you should be able to identify all the knots pictured here: figure 8 follow through, double bowline with Yosemite finish, BHK, bowline, bowline with a bight, figure 8 with a bight, and overhand with a bight.

After reading this text you should be able to identify all the hitches pictured here: Munter hitch, clove hitch, girth hitch, autoblock, and Prusik.

After reading this text you should be able to identify the bends pictured here: double fisherman's and flat overhand.

CHAPTER 2

The Application Heuristic

Climbers are confronted with five essential tasks that require the use of ropework:

1. We need to belay.
2. We need to tie a rope to things (a climber, a tree, a boulder, etc.).
3. We need to anchor (ourselves and our climbing rope).
4. We need to manage the rope when it's not in use.
5. We need to use the rope to manage risk.

Much like so many other aspects of the sport, there are dozens of ways to accomplish each of these tasks with any number of different kinds of ropes, tools, techniques, assistance from others, or knots and hitches. The depth and complexity of the options add to the richness of the sport. It can also be bewildering if we don't have an effective tool for decision making.

This chapter will hopefully equip a climber to make informed choices about the use of the climbing rope. The knots and hitches in this book have each been subjected to the kind of scrutiny and investigation that we suggest all climbers indulge, but the most enduring thing about effective decision making is that it is a flexible tool. We've showcased the knots and hitches in this book because they seem to be the most common solutions to the most frequent contexts that we encounter as rock climbers, climbing instructors, and guides.

However, this chapter also should prepare a climber to work in contexts with which we are unfamiliar. It should provide a tool for deciding whether to use knots and hitches that we have never even heard of. In other words, this chapter should prepare a climber to be a student of the rope, the craft, and the sport. If a reader of this book is simply using the knots and hitches we suggest because we say so, then this chapter, and this entire book, will be an unfortunate failure.

COPE Decision Making

Every time the rope is used, every time a knot or hitch is selected, use the following application heuristic to see if you can COPE with your decision.

Context—What is the context of the ropework?

Options—Given everything I know how to do and all the tools that I have, what are my options?

Pros and Cons—What are the pros and cons of each option?

Experiment—Now that I have made my decision, I'm going to experiment with it to see if my reasoning is sound.

Here is how it works: It all starts with **Context.** Let's say that my friend Derek and I are going sport climbing at a small local crag. There is going to be leading and falling and hang-dogging, and general sport climbing shenanigans. Derek and I want to warm up, push our limits, get totally worked, and eventually succumb to fatigue and the desire for a warm meal. Derek and I are equally skilled AMGA Certified Rock Guides. There doesn't seem to be anyone else at the crag today, so we don't need to serve as role models or mentor anyone. This is our day off. The first rope-related task that I must complete is to tie in to the end of the rope. Context makes a huge difference:

- Sport climbing: likely to load the rope repeatedly and violently with large dynamic loads
- Equally skilled and proficient partner
- No one at the crag to mentor, supervise, or be a role model for

Next, what are my **Options**? I could use a figure 8 follow through or any number of variations on a bowline, or I could clip a figure 8 with a bight with a pair of locking carabiners. The more options I have, the more difficult my decision making will be. But that doesn't mean that I should be afraid of options or difficult decisions. I just need to thoroughly understand the options that I know, and also be willing to forget about the options that are consistently useless. Having climbed a long time and experimented with lots of different knots, I know that these knots are consistently tie-in options:

- Figure 8 follow through
- Double bowline with pass through the harness and a Yosemite finish
- Figure 8 on a bight with a pair of opposite and opposed locking carabiners

What are the **Pros and Cons** of each of those options? If I want to evaluate the pros and cons, then

I need a predictable and fixed set of criteria to evaluate each option. Knots, generally, have five variable qualities:

1. **Strength:** What percentage of material strength will be lost while the knot is in a critical application?

2. **Failure mechanism:** When the knot fails, how does it fail? Does it break the rope? Does it capsize? Does it slip apart?

3. **Security:** How many steps does it take to distort the failure mechanism or reduce the strength of the knot?

4. **Efficiency:** How many steps does it take to tie and untie the knot, how many additional tools are required to accomplish the task, and how much rope is needed to tie the knot?

5. **Visual clarity:** Does my knot look reliable, and is it recognizable from a distance? Does it look goofy, or does it look tight and tidy?

I know the figure 8 follow through is a strong knot. It reduces the strength of the rope by only 10–20 percent in my personal tests, and there are numerous other studies showing comparable strength. But this is also true of a well-tied bowline or the figure 8 on a bight with carabiners.

I know that all three knots fail by breaking the rope.

I know that one gesture of the rope could change the integrity of all three knots, so none of them is any more secure than the next.

In terms of efficiency, the figure 8 with a bight uses two extra carabiners. Those are carabiners that I have to deploy, inspect, and dismantle when I'm done. Instantly, the other two knots seem better.

In a sport climbing context, this knot (figure 8 on a bight with two locking carabiners) wastes carabiners, and it jangles around as I lead. I can't COPE with this knot in this context.

For visual clarity, I can create a mental picture of my figure 8 follow through; Derek and I use this knot all the time when we work together with climbing students. The bowline has a lot of variations that never have the same kind of symmetry.

Given my evaluations of the pros and cons, the figure 8 follow through emerges as my best option. It's time to climb, but remember, this is an **Experiment**. Throughout the use of this knot, I want to be sure that my reasoning is sound.

I climb and I have a great time, but the crux of this climb proves to be more than a little challenging. I probably take ten lobbing lead falls. When I finally lower back to the ground, my aching, tired hands can barely untie the welded knot. If I had selected one of those bowline variations, the knot would have been untied five minutes ago.

Because there is no one else at the crag to mentor, because Derek is just as capable of inspecting my

In a sport climbing context, this figure 8 follow through is going to be difficult to untie if I take repeated falls. Is visual clarity a priority for me today?

Guide's Insight

I remember early in my climbing career, I learned how absolutely strong and durable the belay loop of a harness is constructed to be. I learned that it is stronger than the carabiners we often attach to it, stronger than the climbing rope itself. So I reasoned that I could tie in to it with a climbing rope. In my reasoning, tying in to the belay loop would require less material than passing through the hard points of the harness, it would be easier to visually inspect since the belay loop is not pressed against a climber's body, I could tie in friends without putting my hands too close to their groins, and the belay would be more than strong and durable enough to survive the application. I climbed in this manner for several months, and I explained my reasoning to climbers who quizzed me on the practice. Finally, I met someone who had deliberated on this application longer than I had. She explained to me that the harnesses' hard points were designed to endure the wear and tear of the climbing rope, and that I would someday find a need to keep my belay loop unencumbered and free to clip objects to it. Lastly, she reasoned with me that the harness manufacturer designed the harness to be used in a certain way, and it would be prudent to heed that wisdom. Even though I was attached to my tie-in practice up to that point—I was even proud of it—I had no choice but to amend my practice. My experiment with tying in the belay loop was over.

If all climbers are equally thoughtful and tactful and they discuss best practices and ropework with each other, it is conceivable that our conversation will be more educational and productive. If my knowledgeable friend had chided me too harshly, or used polarizing language to describe my tie-in practice, I might not have been persuaded by her reasoning so quickly. She was respectful enough to listen to me, hear the gap in my reasoning, and offer constructive insights. She never told me I was wrong, or dangerous, or bad, because those absolute terms didn't really capture the nature of my misunderstanding. I wasn't wrong, nor was I particularly dangerous. But I did not have all the information I needed to COPE with my decision. I'm glad she guided me so gracefully, and I think of her when I strive to do the same for others. —RF

bowline as I am, and because ten whippers hopelessly tighten a figure 8 follow through, I'm probably going to pick a double bowline with Yosemite finish on my next lap.

This book is designed to equip climbers to make these choices quickly. As we explore the context of every knot, hitch, bend, and rope management tool, readers should imagine the contexts of their own cliffs, ropes, and climbing teams. Readers should appreciate that in any given context, there are countless ways to solve the problem, and the only way to sort one option out from the next is to have a sound body of knowledge about each knot. A climber should be able to quickly parse out the subtle advantages and disadvantages of each technique and make an informed and reasoned choice. Finally, a good climber does not cling to his/her final decision. A smart climber is always open to an alternative solution that reformulates the heuristic. Or, a smart climber is humble enough to realize that the context can change or it can be misinterpreted. Either way, a smart climber is receptive to the possibility that surviving a task is not a clear indication that he/she has perfected the task.

CHAPTER 3

Tying the Rope to a Climber

One of the most common contexts for ropework in climbing, in many cases the very first task a climber learns, is attaching the rope to a harness. There are many options even for that discrete task, but three knots consistently survive climbers' collective scrutiny and experimentation. As a result, they can be mastered without any need for variation, adjustment, or distortion.

The Figure 8 Follow Through

The figure 8 follow through is one of the most common knots used to attach the rope to a climber's harness. It is the ubiquitous climbing knot because is it strong, easy to recognize from a distance, and easy to teach, and at this point it has permeated climbing culture.

The figure 8 follow through: well dressed, a 6-inch tail, and a small gap between the knot and the harness.

23

Tie the figure 8 knot by creating a loop, wrapping the working end of the rope around the standing end one time, and finally putting the rope end through the original loop.

Run the rope through the tie-in point(s) of a harness.

Use the working end of the rope to retrace the original figure 8. Take care to keep the rope strands parallel in order to tie a well-dressed knot.

Dress the knot by incrementally adjusting all the rope strands. Be sure that all strands are parallel within the knot, the tail is 6 inches (no longer or shorter), and there is a small gap between the knot and the harness.

The Figure 8 Follow Through

Strength: Reduces rope strength by 10-20 percent.

Visual clarity: When tied correctly and well dressed, the figure 8 follow through is unmistakable; its curving parallel lines create a symmetry that no other knot possesses.

Efficiency: It takes only three steps to tie the figure 8 follow through, and it is relatively easy to untie unless it has been heavily loaded.

Security: The figure 8 follow through is a very secure knot. It would require two unlikely contortions to reduce the load-bearing properties of the knot; therefore no secondary knots or hitches are required to secure the figure 8 follow through.

Failure mechanism: The figure 8 follow through has a consistent failure mechanism when large forces are applied to it. It breaks just inside the second turn of its follow through.

Ideal applications: Climbing in a group. Climbing with novices. Climbing instruction.

The Double Bowline with Yosemite Finish

As one of the most complicated knots in this book, the double bowline with a Yosemite finish is a less common way to attach the climbing rope to a climber. But when tied correctly, in an appropriate context (like sport climbing in small teams), or when appropriately supervised, the bowline is a clear and obvious choice.

The double bowline with a Yosemite finish. This odd-looking knot is difficult to recognize from a distance.

Pass the working end of the rope through the tie-in point(s) of the climber's harness.

Create a double loop, such that the standing end of the rope is on the bottom side of the loops and the working end passes into the climber's harness.

Moving from bottom to top, pass the working end through the double loop . . .

. . . under and around the standing end . . .

. . . and back into the double loop.

Pass the tail back through the tie-on point of the harness.

Pass the tail through the bowline's biting tongue.

Finish with an overhand knot, directly in front of the bowline.

The Double Bowline with Yosemite Finish

Strength: A remarkably strong knot. When tied and secured correctly, it reduces material strength by only 10-20 percent.

Visual clarity: The double bowline with a Yosemite finish is an odd-looking knot. If observers are unfamiliar with the knot, it will be difficult for them to tell whether it is tied correctly.

Efficiency: The double bowline with a Yosemite finish requires five separate steps to create, but even after heavy cyclical loads, it is still easy to untie.

Security: The double bowline by itself is an unpredictable knot, but a properly tied backup knot means that it is both secure and predictable. Two separate unlikely contortions of the rope are required to reduce the load-bearing properties of the knot.

Failure mechanism: The double bowline with a Yosemite finish typically breaks right in front of its initial double loop.

Ideal applications: Climbing with experts. Project climbing with lots of falls (easy to untie).

Figure 8 on a Bight

Anyone familiar with a figure 8 follow through will instantly recognize the figure 8 on a bight. Many climbing wall and group climbing programs use this knot with a pair of locking carabiners to attach the climbing rope to one climber after another. When combined with the locking carabiners, the rope can be transferred quickly from one climber to the next, eliminating the need for each climber to tie and untie the knot.

Figure 8 on a Bight

Strength: The figure 8 on a bight has the same strength as the figure 8 follow through.

Visual clarity: The figure 8 on a bight has the same visual clarity as the figure 8 follow through. The carabiners that are necessarily used with the knot are also easy to inspect.

Efficiency: Efficiency is the entire reason to use the figure 8 on a bight. It can be tied once, with the same carabiners attached and reused for each climber. However, at the end of the climb, the knot will have been loaded repeatedly, sometimes heavily. As a result, it will be more difficult to untie.

The **security** and **failure mechanisms** of this knot are the same as those of the figure 8 follow through.

Ideal applications: Climbing in a group. Climbing with novices. Climbing instruction where time is limited. The attachment can be pre-rigged in advance and eliminate knot teaching.

Two opposite and opposed locking carabiners are advisable when attaching the figure 8 on a bight to a climber's harness.

Tying the figure 8 with a bight is simple. Find an adequately sized bight of rope.

Tie a figure 8 knot with a bight of rope instead of a single strand using the same steps.

Variations and Distortions

There are limitless variations on the three knots presented in this chapter. Most of the time, however, those variations do not consistently survive the Experiment phase of our application heuristic. Here are a few examples.

Tying a double overhand or barrel knot in front of the figure 8 follow through does not alter the failure mechanism of the knot. It simply adds another step to an already secure knot.

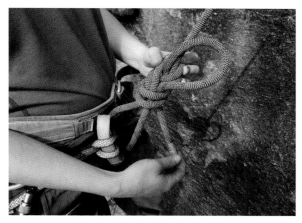

Tracing the tail of the figure 8 follow through back through the knot, known as the Yosemite finish, Kentucky tucky, or Tennessee tuck, distorts the visual clarity of the knot while failing to increase the knot's strength or security. Since the result is already visually unclear, the double bowline seems advantageous, being easier to untie.

The BHK is often selected to connect carabiners to a harness because it is a redundant knot and mirrors the redundant carabiners. However, this bulky, obtrusive knot defaults to a nonredundant climbing rope, undermining the selection of the knot.

Guide's Insight

At the North Carolina Outward Bound School, where I spend much of my year teaching students and staff to rock climb, one of our core educational pillars is to teach the students the value of craftsmanship. In all of their pursuits, but especially in rock climbing, we teach students that details, care, and precision matter. Tying the figure 8 follow through is no exception. Students groan and complain as they are continually prodded to tie the figure 8 follow through in a standardized manner: a small gap between the knot and the harness, a 6-inch tail, and a perfectly dressed and symmetrical knot. Interestingly enough, with our insistence that they do so, students quickly tie the knot correctly out of habit, just like a professional guide.

I am reminded of this fact when I see climbers not take the extra time to make their figure 8 follow throughs just right. Not only does a messy knot contradict the reason we pick the knot in the first place, but it takes only a few seconds to correct it. Furthermore, if all climbers just got in the habit of tying it right in the first place, there would never be a need to adjust it. If hundreds of teenage Outward Bound students can do it summer after summer, I'm convinced that anyone can do it with only the slightest effort. —RF

CHAPTER 4

Tying the Rope to Other Things

Tying the rope to a climber is a familiar and predictable task. No matter how big or small a climber may be, the amount of rope needed for tying in is consistent. But when the rope is tied around some other object, the amount of rope needed can vary, there is not always a rope end to work with, and there is often a need to create redundancy in the attachment.

Consider the task of tying the rope around trees. Some trees are gigantic, requiring an expansive circumference of rope. Some trees have sharp and abrasive bark, so running two strands of material around the tree seems more durable. Sometimes climbers are setting up multiple anchors with the same rope, so the rope ends are not available. It is important, therefore, to learn to work with sections of the middle of a rope, or a bight.

We might imagine similar circumstances for all objects, everything from trees to boulders to flagpoles and fence posts. In each case, the bowline, the bowline with a bight, and the use of slings and cordellette give enough options to connect a rope to almost anything.

Bowline

When a rope end is available, the bowline is the most obvious choice for attaching the rope to an object.

Unlike a figure 8 follow through, the bowline does not have a preliminary step that isolates the distance between the end of the rope and the place where the knot will eventually reside. When tying the bowline, one can circumnavigate an object of any size, and then tie the knot in any proximity to the object.

A bowline with a backup knot tied to a tree. A precise amount of rope is being used because tying the bowline is an efficient process, in terms of time and material.

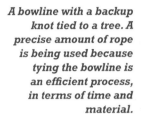

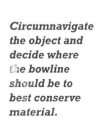

Circumnavigate the object and decide where the bowline should be to best conserve material.

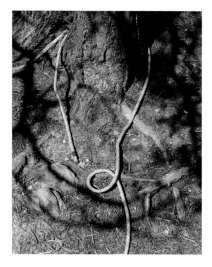

Start with a loop.

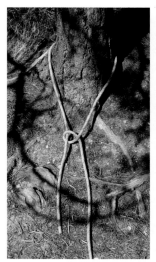

Pass the tail out of the loop . . .

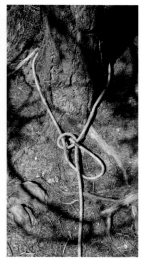

. . . under and around the standing end, and back into the loop.

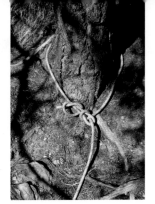

Finish with a backup knot, positioned directly beside the initial loop.

Bowline

Strength: The bowline is a strong knot. When tied correctly with a backup knot, it reduces the material strength by only 10-20 percent.

Visual clarity: The bowline has a distinctive shape, but when it's upside down or when any of its distinctive loops are not tight enough, it is more difficult to recognize.

Efficiency: There are only three steps to tying a bowline, and even after heavy cyclical loads, it is not too difficult to untie.

Security: The bowline can behave erratically in response to cyclical dynamic loads. If the tail that protrudes from the knot is too short, it is possible to make the knot slip apart or unravel. Otherwise, the knot will break in front of the first biting loop. Applying a backup knot makes the knot behave more consistently.

Failure mechanism: When tied with a backup knot, the bowline will break when it fails.

Ideal application: The bowline is ideal for tying the end of a rope around objects of varying sizes.

Bowline with a Bight

It is particularly advantageous to know how to tie a bowline with a bight of rope. In the construction of many anchors, the rope end may be preoccupied, so the anchor may need to be tied around objects with a remaining bight of rope. It is also commonly the case that a bowline with a bight proves to be more durable when tied around abrasive objects because two strands of rope end up rubbing against the object instead of one.

Properties: A bowline with a bight can be regarded as having twice the strength of a bowline in a single strand. It is weakening the material strength of two strands of rope instead of just one. Similarly, its security and failure mechanisms mirror those of the bowline in a single strand, but twice the load is needed to create those failures and insecurities. As a result, it is just as important to tie a backup knot. In terms of efficiency, the bowline with a bight uses twice as much material to circumnavigate an object as a bowline with a rope end.

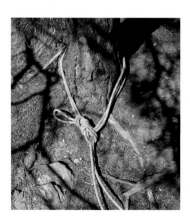

Essentially a bowline with two strands of material, a bowline with a bight is a redundant knot with twice the strength of its single-strand counterpart.

Circumnavigate the object with a bight of rope.

Make a loop with a bight.

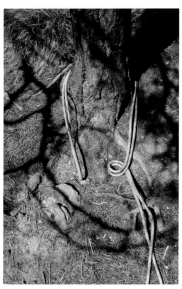

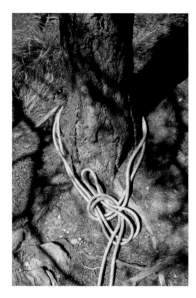

Pass the original bight through the loop, under and around the standing bight, and back into the original loop.

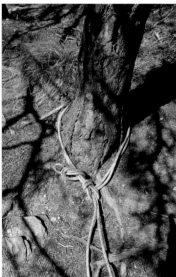

Finish with a backup knot.

Slings and Cordellette

Slings and cordellette, combined with locking carabiners, are also handy ways to attach a rope to an
object. If the object is small enough for a 48-inch
sling or cordellette to enwrap it, a locking carabiner
and a figure 8 with a bight can be used to attach the
rope to the object. As soon as slings, carabiners, ropes,
and cordellette become enchained, it is important to
remember that the strength of a given knot, or of any
link in the chain, is always relative to the weakest link
in the system. Strong knots in strong ropes become
irrelevant if they are attached to poorly tied slings,
open carabiners, or weak objects.

Basketing

Basketing is simply looping a
sling around an object and using
a carabiner to close the loop.
Basketing does not require any
knot or hitch, which not only is
efficient, but also means that the
material strength is not weak-
ened by any knot.

*A basketed sling
or cordellette
retains its material
strength as long
as the object is
not too sharp.
Also, triaxial loads
can be avoided
if the basketed
object has a
relatively small
circumference.*

*Double up:
A quick
overhand
knot creates
material
redundancy
in a
basketed
sling.*

Basket hitch with a handle: The surgeon's knot spreads more surface contact onto an object but does not constrict the object. As a result, it is a more durable option for the sling and the object, and it can eliminate the possibility of a triaxial load on the carabiner.

Surgeon's Knot

On some objects, like trees, a basketed sling can slide down the object, which can be abrasive or alter the way the object is meant to be loaded. In these instances, a surgeon's knot is a less destructive way to attach a sling or cordellette to an object. It adds friction and stickiness to help keep the sling in place and loaded in the desired fashion.

Girth Hitch

The girth hitch is one of the most commonly used methods for attaching a sling or cordellette to an

A girth hitch constricts the object it is hitched to. It thereby reduces material strength and should be used carefully and selectively. Keep it open and less binding as pictured.

object. But it is a destructive hitch, and its application can greatly reduce the material strength. There is
almost never an occasion where the application of this
hitch does not have a perfectly viable alternative, like a
basket or surgeon's knot.

Guide's Insight

When I teach aspiring professionals to build
toproping anchors, I try to help them see that
the aesthetic qualities of an anchor make a difference. How does it look? Does it look elegant?

Interestingly, AMGA-Certified Single Pitch
Instructors can recognize elegance when they
see it, and so can their students. At first, however, it can be difficult for them to explain or
qualify what exactly makes an anchor look
elegant. There are a few things: the precise use
of anchoring materials, no material wasted, no
carabiner or tool wasted when a knot would suffice, and the visually pleasing sight of one rope
used to connect all the components and create
a master point. The more familiar anchor builders become with the bowline and the bowline
with a bight, the more elegant their anchors will
become. Eventually, any toproping team can
create anchors that have the same signature
elegance and efficiency as those made by an
AMGA Certified Single Pitch Instructor.

CHAPTER 5

Using the Rope for Anchoring

If a rope can be tied to several objects, it can easily be used to create an anchor. The difference between simply tying a rope to an object and building an anchor is that an anchor is a system used to safeguard life and limb. Since the purpose of this text is to focus on knots and hitches and the application of the rope, a lengthy discussion of anchoring could be distracting.

We shall assume, therefore, that the fundamental principles that should apply to all climbing anchors will apply to those presented in this chapter. They will be adequately strong to sustain all potential loads in the climbing system. So the components used to construct the anchor are assumed to be living trees, well-situated and sturdy boulders, strong and correctly placed bolts in good rock, or well-placed artificial/removable protection. The anchor should be redundant and distribute load intelligently to the components.

A static setup rope is an excellent tool for building anchors that accomplish all these tasks when the components are far apart from each other. A cordelette or sling is a great tool when the components are closer together.

Bowline, Bowline with a Bight, and the BHK

The BHK is an excellent way to combine the load-bearing potential of trees and boulders. It is easy to tie, and unlike any of the other knots one might tie with a bight of rope, the BHK has material redundancy. Anchor systems rely on a system of redundancy right up to the master point, and the redundancy is just as important in the knot that creates the master point as it is in the rest of the system.

The combination of a bowline, a bowline with a bight, and the BHK is one of the most versatile anchoring techniques.

The BHK is tied by turning a single bight of rope into a double bight.

Then an overhand on a bight is tied with two strands of material, creating a redundant knot.

The resulting loop can be managed by clipping back into the master point.

Because slings and cordellette are attached to components in a closed loop, a quick overhand knot creates the redundant BHK. There is no loop to manage in this case.

Slings, Cordellette, and the BHK

Cordellettes and slings can easily be brought together in much the same manner as a static rope, but an overhand knot that is tied with double strands of material is a redundant knot, without any extra effort required.

Sling with Load-Limiting Overhand Knots: The Magic X

When load-limiting overhand knots are added to a sliding/magic X anchor configuration, the result is a

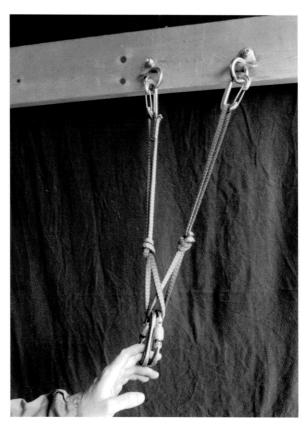

Tying two overhand knots in line, on a sling or cordellette, allows anchor builders to use the magic X anchor more convincingly. It is now redundant, and extension potential has been greatly limited.

redundant, self-adjusting, and strong system. However, in Spectra or Dyneema slings, these load-limiting knots can be difficult to untie after sustained cyclical loads, like the kinds of loads applied by a toprope.

Doubled Cordellette with Load-Limiting Overhand Knots: The Quad

When load-limiting overhand knots are tied into a doubled-over cordellette or extra-long sling, the result is also a redundant, self-adjusting, and strong anchoring system. Unlike a sling, the load-limiting overhand knots tied into the quad are composed of four strands of cordellette. The bulkier overhand knot is usually easier to untie after sustained cyclical loads.

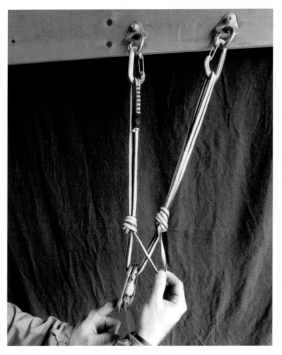

A doubled-over cordellette or long sling with knots can configure the quad. By clipping three of the four master point strands, a failure of one anchor point will not result in total failure.

The Clove Hitch

The clove hitch is not necessarily used to construct an anchor, but it is clearly an anchoring hitch. The clove hitch is used to attach a section of climbing rope to a locking carabiner, but unlike the figure 8 follow through, the clove hitch can be quickly adjusted to

The Clove Hitch

Strength: The clove hitch is a slippery hitch, and it can behave erratically at high loads, when the rope is wet, or when interacting with different carabiners. It might be helpful to imagine the clove hitch as having the potential to slip at 1,000 pounds. Actual strength can be quite variable, so low loads (like a climber's body weight) are most appropriate for the clove hitch.

Visual clarity: The clove hitch's capturing strand is easily recognizable.

Efficiency: It takes only three quick steps to tie a clove hitch, and even after heavy loads it will slide off of its locking carabiner.

Security: As long as the load applied to the clove hitch remains constant and unidirectional, it is quite reliable. However, dynamic loads, D-shaped carabiners, and wet/icy conditions can make the clove hitch less secure.

Failure mechanism: The clove can fail in a variety of ways. High dynamic loads can cause the rope to break right in front of the hitch, whereas slower tensile loads can cause the hitch to slip.

Ideal application: Anchoring the climber/belayer to an anchor with a locking carabiner.

The clove hitch functions most consistently when tied to an HMS or a pear-shaped carabiner.

shorten or elongate the distance between the hitch and the climber. Unlike anchor connections with a PAS/Chain Reactor (daisy link) or daisy chain, a clove hitch can be measured to the exact distance a climber may need to stay secured at cliff's edge. The clove hitch is best used on an HMS or a pear-shaped carabiner.

To tie the clove hitch, form a loop.

Form a second loop, right beside the first one in exactly the same manner, which will result in the working and standing ends of the rope on opposite sides of a biting strand.

"Scissor" the two loops, so that the working and standing ends are pinned against the carabiner by the biting strand.

Biting Loop

Adjusting the clove hitch. Unseating the biting loop allows a climber to create or take up slack on the standing or working end of the hitch, without unlocking the carabiner or retying the hitch.

Guide's Insight

A former climbing partner of mine sent me a photo from my early days of climbing. In the photo I have arrived at the top of a climb, elated and pleased with myself. My friend, however, uses the photo to point out my use of a daisy chain. In those days I used the daisy chain, permanently attached to my harness, anytime I needed to anchor. I knew the clove, but I never understood its utility.

Today, I am such a vehement advocate of the clove hitch that it is hard to remember those daisy chain days, so my friend likes to remind me where I came from. But I do remember how I became convinced that the clove hitch was a better option. The application heuristic showed me that I had become attached to the daisy chain without thought or consideration. As a result, I assumed that the limitations (limited adjustability, manufacturer's recommended use, and fairly short length) of that tool were inherent difficulties of the sport.

That is not true, of course. When I began to COPE with the clove hitch and the occasional use of a sling, I felt more secure, I was always in a better position to observe the second climber, and my photos were less indicative of my lack of knowledge.

CHAPTER 6

Using the Rope to Belay

When belaying, climbers either coordinate the rope with some sort of belay/rappel device and a locking carabiner, or they rely on a belay hitch (the Munter hitch) and a locking carabiner. This pattern is entirely appropriate, so there are a number of knots that all belayers need to learn in order to perform belay tasks completely. Any belayer should know how to close a belay device in order to let go of the brake hand, and there are a few different knots that will allow him/her to do this. Any belayer also should know how use a Munter hitch, as it is an effective belay, requires minimal equipment, and provides a smooth and effective way for belayers to move a rope in both directions (taking in slack and lowering).

Going Hands Free on a Plate/ Aperture/Tuber Belay Device

An ATC, a Reverso, and any number of other plate belay devices (including the original Sticht plate) require a fairly tricky knot known as the mule knot. Traditionally, the mule knot has been tied in a configuration that avoids the spine of the attachment carabiner. As a result, it is cumbersome to tie and difficult to reduce in a precise manner. The following version of the mule knot avoids those difficulties entirely, but the initial slipknot functions best when the attachment carabiner is an adequately sized HMS or pear-shaped locking carabiner.

If tied correctly, the mule knot tends to constrict upon itself and will break in front of the initial slip-knot only at very high loads. As a result, it is a reliable and secure way for a belayer to secure a climber when the brake hand is needed to perform some auxiliary task.

Mule knot for a plate/aperture belay device.

Carefully pull a bight of the brake strand through the locking carabiner.

Push a slipknot through the bight from the standing end of the brake strand.

Elongate the resulting loop, and use an overhand with a bight, in front of the belay device around the load strand, to close the knot.

The Munter Hitch

There is a checkered history behind the Munter hitch, and its original source is in some historic dispute. Whether Werner Munter invented the hitch or merely

To tie the Munter hitch, create a loop of rope.

Form a second loop right beside the first one in exactly the same manner, which will result in the working and standing ends of the rope on opposite sides of a biting strand.

Fold, or "taco," the two loops before placing them in the carabiner.

The "tongue" of the Munter hitch always points toward the direction the rope is travelling. Here the tongue points to the climber, because the belayer is giving slack.

Here the tongue points to the brake hand, because the belayer is taking in slack.

popularized it, whether it was devised by German mountaineers or Italian sailors, American climbers most commonly refer to the hitch as the Munter. Climbers have learned that the friction the hitch applies to rope easily augments the holding power of their gripped hands. But, like any belay system, the strength of the Munter is relative to the strength of the hand that is holding it.

Going Hands Free with a Munter Hitch: The Munter–Mule Knot

Just like the belayer who needs to go hands free while using a plate/aperture/tuber belay device, the Munter hitch belayer will need to be able to close the Munter hitch with yet another version of the mule knot.

The Munter-mule knot begins with the Munter loaded. The tongue should be pointing toward the climber.

Carefully create a loop in the brake strand.

Use the standing end of the brake strand to create a slipknot that captures the brake strand and the load strand.

Tie off the resulting loop with an overhand with a bight around the loaded strand of the rope.

The Munter-mule knot is also commonly applied as a releasable attachment during improvised rescue sequences, load transfers, and institutional rappel rigging. If a belayer learns to tie the Munter-mule knot as a simple hands-free belay application, he/she will be well prepared when the knot needs to be applied to more complex rigging and rescue scenarios.

A Note about Load Strands and Carabiner Spines

There has been much written about load strands of the clove hitch and Munter hitch and their positioning relative to the spine or gate side of a carabiner. To simplify the issues, the following maxim has become somewhat entrenched: Always put the load strand on the spine side of a carabiner. However, thousands of anecdotal incidents, whether intentional or otherwise, seem to dispute the absolute necessity of this old maxim.

A more accurate perception of the problem might sound something like this: Use carabiners that are appropriate for hitches, when tying and using hitches. The ideal carabiner for hitches in 5mm to 11mm cords and ropes is an HMS or pear-shaped carabiner. Locking D-shaped carabiners do not have a wide basket or basin, and therefore the behavior of the clove and Munter can be more problematic. The Munter hitch has a hard time rotating back and forth through such a small carabiner. The clove can lose much of its holding power if the load strand of the hitch is not situated on the spine side of the smaller carabiner. So the problem with load strands and spine sides has more to do with carabiner selection than any inherent weaknesses in the hitches. Keep these realities in mind if, at some point, there are no HMS or pear-shaped carabiners left on the planet. We will have to adhere to those old dogmas more rigidly in that case.

Going Hands Free on a GriGri or Other Assisted Braking Device (ABD)

The assisted braking mechanism of a GriGri has proven itself to be deceptively reliable. So reliable, in fact, that many climbers trust it absolutely, thought-lessly relinquishing the brake hand once the braking cam is firmly engaged. This practice is a misuse of the GriGri, however. Instead, an overhand on a bight knot should be tied in close proximity to the device,

A quick overhand with a bight in the brake strand, directly beside the GriGri, is an adequate way to secure the GriGri.

if the belayer wishes to relinquish his/her brake hand. Doing so guarantees that any interference with the braking cam's range of motion will not endanger the climber.

Guide's Insight

When I first began to climb, I didn't see why I needed to understand such a finicky and awkward knot as the mule. It seemed obvious to me that if I ever needed to let go of the brake strand while using an ATC, I could just tie an overhand knot and let that knot jam against the belay plate. When rappelling, I had learned to use a leg wrap to go hands free. I did not understand why the mule knot was insisted upon. When I began to mentor others, and eventually to teach climbing professionally, I discovered that it is not always that easy to get the climber's weight off the rope, and sometimes belayers don't want the climber's weight to shift a single inch. When I was rappelling, I discovered a need for a more secure closure of a rappel system, so the leg wrap didn't seem as practicable anymore. As the contexts of my climbing deepened and became more complicated, the mule knot emerged as the best way to close a belay.

If I had learned to use the knot in the first place, I might have avoided the day when a good friend dangled off of Pilot Mountain while I attempted to dislodge an overhand with a bight from my ATC. I might have been more secure as I swung back and forth, cleaning quickdraws as a leg-wrapped rappel constricted my thigh. But, mostly, I might not have looked, to all observers and fellow climbers, like such a total goofball. —RF

Using the Rope to Manage Risk

A wide variety of knots have miscellaneous applications as backups, safety precautions, use in rescue systems, or other best practices. It would be difficult to fully elucidate every one of these knots and hitches in this book, and ultimately some knots and hitches seem to be more useful than others. Even though there are dozens of options for doing so, climbers generally need a group of knots to close the climbing system, back up a rappel or a lower, create a tether or rappel extension, and grab any section of rope that may already be taut.

Closing the System: Overhand with a Bight

In a typical toproping activity or a rappel, there is always at least one free rope end available. When toproping, the climber is tied to one end of the rope while the other end of the rope is left free. In rappelling, the rope is either fixed, in which case one end is affixed to an anchor while the other is on the ground, or the middle of the rope is running through an anchor with both ends on the ground. Through a variety of circumstances and awkward scenarios, climbers have managed to rappel off the ends of ropes, or lower each other off the ends of ropes. So a habit

The overhand with a bight closing a belay system.

The overhand with a bight closing a rappel system.

of "closing the system," or managing both ends of the rope, is both prudent and proven. A simple knot in the end of the rope is one of the easiest and most timely ways to accomplish this task. A knot that has bulk enough to jam against a belay device or hitch, a knot that is secure even getting tossed down from a cliff's edge, and a knot that is easy to recognize as it dangles beneath a rappeler, or hides in a rope stack, is essential. So the overhand with a bight is a satisfactory choice.

Closing the System: Ground Anchor and Clove Hitch

Since ground anchors are also a routine part of toproping with novice belayers or among climbers with severe weight disparities, it is advantageous and efficient to use the climbing rope as a ground anchoring tool. If the climber is tied to one end of the rope, the belayer can tie in to the other end; the figure 8 follow through seems like an appropriate choice in this context. Now the belayer has the option to attach the climbing rope to any large object via a locking carabiner and a clove hitch. Since a ground anchor essentially offers ballast to a belayer, smaller boulders, a cluster of backpacks, or smaller trees are good options. Often, a third climber can be used. The adjustable clove hitch will allow the belayer to cinch in line with the ground anchor and the top anchor.

Here, the belayer is ground anchored with a figure 8 follow through and a clove hitch. A versatile way to ground anchor, it also closes the system.

Extensions and Tethers: Extending the Belay Loop

Climbers often need an anchoring tool other than the climbing rope itself, like when cleaning a sport climb or doing a multistage rappel or descent. It is possible in all of these scenarios to clip the belay loop directly into a master point with a locking carabiner. However, such a small distance between the climber's body and the anchor is often unmanageable. So climbers have learned to create an extension of the belay loop that has the same essential properties: a redundant construction and monolithic strength (stronger than any conceivable force the climbing system could create). With such a task in mind, the 48-inch sling proves itself to be apt. Basketing a 48-inch sling through the hard points of the harness and closing the basket with an overhand knot creates an attachment point that is materially redundant and has at least 30kN of strength, just like the belay loop.

The use of a double-length sling can create an attachment point that has the same essential properties as a belay loop: strength and redundancy.

Extensions and Tethers: The Girth Hitch

When the extended belay loop configuration is not an option, climbers may need to use any number of other materials to create an extension or a tether. A shoulder-length sling, for example, is too short to basket through the harness and then tie an overhand knot. Similarly, the extended belay loop may still be too short to allow the climber to stand up straight at a cliff's edge. In these contexts a climber may elect to use a girth hitch. However, the girth hitch should be used with great caution. In failure tests it can behave erratically. Sometimes slight twists or rotations of the hitch can drastically reduce the material strength of the tether, up to 75 percent in some cases. Usually these applications are not a concern because climbers are applying only low loads to the hitch (body weight), or they are using the hitch simply to back

The girth hitch can be used to attach a personal tether, but the tether will not have the same essential properties as a belay loop. It is weaker and not redundant.

up an otherwise secure stance on a ledge. However, anytime there are potential shock loads on the hitch or large loads applied to it, the girth hitch is not a prudent option.

Backups for Rappels and Lowers: The Autoblock

The autoblock consistently survives the application heuristic in the most common climbing applications because it is quick and easy to tie/untie, and it uses up all the material (making a tidy and compact hitch). Other classic friction hitches like the Prusik or the kleimheist do not have these same characteristics. They are cumbersome to tie and dress, they grip the rope too tightly, and they are difficult to remove after heavy loads. When lowering or rappelling, climbers only need a friction that is as strong as their grip strength, so the

Clip the accessory cord loop into a locking carabiner attached to the belay loop. Take care to position the cord's joining knot near the carabiner.

Enwrap the brake strand(s) of the rope as many times as the accessory cord loop is long.

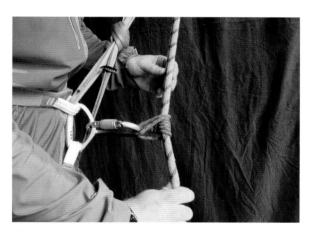

Clip the accessory cord loop back into the locking carabiner and lock it.

autoblock more than meets the task. It slides along smoothly and engages only if the climber becomes incapacitated. Once the lower or rappel is over, the

Rappelling in this manner utilizes an extension of the belay loop and an autoblock backup. Many incidents in North American rappelling could have been averted by this kind of setup.

autoblock can be quickly deconstructed and stowed for future use. In the case of the lower and the rappel, it is prudent to use a locking carabiner to attach the autoblock to the belay loop, and a 5mm nylon loop is an effective size and diameter for hitching to most climbing ropes and static ropes.

The Classic Friction Hitch:
The Prusik

We'd be remiss not to mention the Prusik, but its ideal applications involve rescue/assistance procedures that are both rare and difficult to describe in this text. However, there are clearly instances where the Prusik survives the application heuristic ahead of its peers. In an ascension system, in a haul system, in a belay escape, and in a load transfer, a Prusik grips the rope tightly and predictably. In some tests the Prusik grips the rope so tightly that high loads actually strip the sheath off of the rope. However, in the most common applications of a friction hitch in climbing (backing up rappels and lowers), the Prusik is overly tedious to tie/untie and its great strength is not needed.

Still a mainstay in climbing, the Prusik is best applied when maximum grabbing power is needed.

In the process of enwrapping the rope, loop the Prusik loop through itself three times. Be sure the joining knot does not interfere with the wraps or the clipping point to carabiner.

Be sure each wrap of the Prusik is parallel, without twists.

Guide's Insight

When I first learned to COPE with an autoblock for rappelling and lowering backups, I tried to quantify my admiration for the hitch. Here's what I came up with: It takes me three seconds longer to tie a Prusik than an autoblock on average. It takes me one second longer to untie and stow it on average. When lowering or backing up a rappel, the Prusik results in two seconds of "hassles" for every one in ten lowers or rappels, because it grabs too tightly and has to be wrestled free from constriction.

Every year, I spend about 210 days on the rock, either working or recreating. An average outing consists of 600 feet of climbing, adding up short climbs and averaging them with long climbs, short days with long days. Let's call it six rappels and three lowers per outing, because the lowers are less frequent.

$9 \times 210 = 1{,}890$ uses of friction hitch backup for rappels and lowers

$(1{,}890 \text{ Prusik ties} \times 3 \text{ seconds}) + (1{,}890 \text{ Prusik unties} \times 1 \text{ second}) = 7{,}560 \text{ seconds}$

Even if I managed to have zero hassles all year with the Prusik, it would still cost me two hours and six minutes every year. That could be an exotic meal with my wife one night, and beer with my friends the next night.

Thanks to the autoblock, I get to have an exotic meal with my wife and beer with my friends once a year. I earned it! —RF

CHAPTER 8

Managing the Rope

A 60m or 70m rope can be an unwieldy and chaotic mess if it is not properly managed. The slipknot is almost always the culprit. As a rope unfurls from its pile or its coils, it is perfectly natural for one bight of the rope to be pulled through an incidental loop in the stack or the pile. As one clustered slipknot mingles with the rest of the pile, slipknots can naturally be created within slipknots, and so the mess begins. Thankfully, the rope can be managed with a few simple techniques.

In this chapter we will discuss flaking a rope out for its initial use, techniques for managing a rope while belaying, and coiling a rope for transport.

Flaking a Rope

The initial treatment of a rope is an important step. It has a few important purposes. First, a rope that has been transported in a rope bag or bucket, or even in a tight single-strand coil, is not guaranteed to pay out smoothly to a belayer. Flaking a rope prepares it for use. Second, flaking provides an opportunity for the climbing team to inspect (visually and physically) every inch of the rope. Severe abrasion in the sheath, exposure of core strands, breaks, gaps, and weaknesses all should be avoided. So flaking a rope is a logical time to find any signs of rope damage. Lastly, flaking a rope allows the climbing team to retrieve the rope ends, which they will need in order to tie in and close the system.

Rope Stack

Carefully stacking the rope in a tight, tidy pile is one of the quickest and most effective ways to manage the rope. The tighter the pile, the less surface area the loops of the rope spread out over, and the less likely incidental slipknots are to occur. It is important to remember that both ends will likely be needed at some point to tie in or close the system; so keep the ends where they can be quickly retrieved. Also, remember that a tight rope pile now has a top and a bottom. Rope should unfurl in an orderly manner from the top of the pile, but not necessarily from the bottom. If a ledge, flat section of terrain, or slab is available, rope stacking is an obvious choice for managing a rope.

This neatly stacked rope feeds smoothly and can easily be moved from one place to another.

Lap Coils

Climbers do not always have the most capacious ledges available to stack a rope. They are often at a hanging stance as they attempt to manage the rope. So coiling the rope in long loops over the belayer's tie-in can be a good way to manage the rope. But these coils must be precisely placed, and if they are not done carefully, they create more problems than they solve. Be certain a rope stack is not an option before taking the time and care needed to establish lap coils.

The length of each lap coil can make the task more efficient. Long loops mean fewer of them. But if the long loops get entangled in terrain, are blown about by wind, or interfere with other climbers, they are not a good option. Shorter coils become necessary

These lap coils are neatly arranged on the belayer's tie-in. Each concentric loop is slightly smaller to guarantee a smooth rope feed.

Here, the lap coils have simply been hung from the anchor in a basketed sling.

in any of those instances. But shorter coils take more time and require even more care. To avoid slipknots each consecutive coil should be slightly shorter than the coil that preceded it. Shorter coils necessitate shorter and shorter increments between each coil, making management time consuming. Make no mistake, however: the extra time needed to manage coils carefully is almost always worth it.

New England Coil

When the rope is simply being transported from one place to the next, stowing it into a durable and closed coil is important. The use of rope bags and buckets might make transport quick and easy, but rope coiling is an important part of learning to use a rope.

The New England coil wraps the rope in single strands, so they can easily be deployed into an initial rope stack at the base of a climb. There is no need to keep track of the initial rope end once all the coils are aligned. The entire closure involves the final rope stack. And the shape of the coil means that the rope can be carried under the brain of a backpack or between a climber's head and the backpack (sitting atop the backpack straps).

To form a New England coil, fold single strands of the rope back and forth across your neck and shoulders. Each loop should be the same size as the previous loop.

With 5 feet left until the tail, take the coils in hand and create a Z capture with the standing end of the tail.

Wrap the tail around the entire coil to pin the Z capture.

The Z capture pins the tail against the wraps, and it can be formed without retrieving the other end of the rope.

Mountaineer's Coil

The mountaineer's coil is a classic-looking coil, and it is still the most comfortable way to carry a rope without a backpack. The wide coils ride comfortably over one shoulder, without creating a 9–10mm pressure point on the shoulders. But the mountaineer's coil is more time consuming because it has to be uncoiled one strand at a time, just as it was coiled. If not, the concentric loops can easily create the most heinous nightmare of consecutive slipknots imaginable.

The size of the consecutive loops in a mountaineer's coil is important. Each loop should be no longer or shorter than the distance between the shoulder and the hip of the person who intends to carry the coil. Coils that are too long create snagging and tripping hazards. Coils that are too short are uncomfortable to carry.

In concentric circles, form the mountaineer's coil between your neck/shoulders and an extended hand.

With 3 feet of tail left, take the coils in hand.

Form an N capture with the standing end of the rope.

Wrap the 3-foot tail around the coils, pinning the N capture.

The N capture pins the tail against all the wraps.

Join the last segments of the tails with a square knot.

Double Butterfly Coil

The quickest way to coil rope, when simple speed is an absolute priority, is the double butterfly coil. Since it enwraps two strands of rope as it coils, it is twice as fast as any alternative method. However, since the rope is aligned at the rope ends to start and stacks all the subsequent wraps accordingly, it can cause more frequent slipknots during the uncoiling/pre-climb rope stacking process. Usually this is not a tremendous encumbrance, but this process is almost always less timely than a rope that initially coiled with single strands. As a result, a double butterfly coil might be a great choice when making a quick retreat from a climb, when the rope will no longer be needed during the climbing outing, and when time is a factor.

Find the tails of the rope and set 8 feet aside.

Moving both strands of the rope, fold the rope across the neck and shoulders, being certain that each loop is the same length.

Holding the coils in hand, enwrap them with the two tails that were originally set aside.

With 4 feet remaining, pass a bight of the tails through the head of the coil, and girth hitch the tails through themselves.

If the tails of the butterfly coil are strategically long enough, it can be carried for a short distance like a backpack.

Joining Knots (Bends)

I t is not uncommon to join the ends of ropes, cords, or webbing. If the rope ends being joined are within 1 mm of each other's diameter, the application heuristic really hinges on one key question: Is the union permanent or temporary? If the joining knot is permanent, climbers should seek the strongest, most secure knot available, one that is easily recognizable, with a predictable failure mechanism. If the joining knot is temporary, then it might be worth considering the efficiency of the knot. Some joining knots are so difficult to untie after being loaded that climbers should rightfully consider a knot that is simply strong and secure enough to sustain all the potential loads applied to it.

Double Fisherman's

The double fisherman's is one of the strongest and most secure joining knots available to rock climbers. When tied correctly, its four parallel loops and crossing strands are also unmistakable. At high loads the knot tends to break right in front of the first loop. However, the double fisherman's has to be meticulously tied to get it just right, and after modest loads (like a rappelling body weight) it can be arduous and time consuming to untie.

To begin the double fisherman's, ensure that the joining strands are moving in opposite directions.

Take the strand that is pointing right, and double overhand it from left to right.

The opposite strand will therefore be pointing left, so double overhang it from right to left.

To finish the double fisherman's, dress and stress both tails, then pull them together. The double overhangs should fit like puzzle pieces on one side and have four parallel strands on the other.

Therefore it is an ideal knot for joining rope ends that climbers never intend to untie, like accessory cord loops, cordellettes, or gear slings. Two inches of tail on each side of the knot gives the double fisherman's adequate security.

Flat Overhand

The flat overhand is not as strong a knot as any number of other joining knots. It can be made to capsize at loads that are less than 30 percent of the rope's strength. For this reason the flat overhand often carries the unfair moniker "European death knot (EDK)." However, when tied correctly, the flat overhand excels as a joining knot because it is easy to tie, easy to inspect, and easy to untie after use. The weaknesses of the knot are easy to understand and mitigate by tying at least 12 inches of tails in front of the knot (which makes consecutive capsizing unlikely), dressing the knot correctly, and applying smaller body weight loads to the knot.

Therefore the flat overhand is an ideal knot for temporarily joining two rope ends, especially when body weight loads are the only loads applied to the knot.

Guide's Insight

Much like my preference for the autoblock in rappelling and lowering applications, selecting the flat overhand to join ropes for rappelling is quite a time-saver.

Last year, I earned a trip to coastal North Carolina to visit my family. —RF

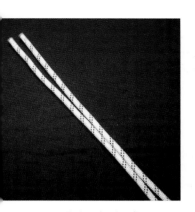

To begin the flat overhand, align the rope ends.

At 12 inches from the ends of the ropes, tie an overhand knot with both strands.

To prevent premature capsizing, individually tighten each strand into the knot and ensure that the knot is well dressed.

Water Knot

Many climbers still insist on using 1-inch tubular nylon webbing to construct shoulder-length and double-length slings. There is an obvious incentive to do so because these kinds of slings are much cheaper than a manufactured sling. Of course, the trade-off is that climbers will have to select a joining knot to make the slings. They will have to tie the joining knot correctly and inspect the knot every time it is used. The mandatory diligence required by these knots often makes the price point on a manufactured sling more attractive.

Nevertheless, the water knot is still a part of climbing culture, and it is encountered so regularly in climbing circles, old and young, that it bears mentioning. The water knot is a strong knot, and the pattern of tying one overhand knot in one end of the webbing, then retracing that knot with the other end in the opposite direction, is easy to remember and recognize. As long as the tails of the water knot are at least 2 inches long, it tends break right in front of the first loop under high loads. But the smooth, flat webbing and the nature of slings being crammed in and out of backpacks and stuff sacks means that water knots can slowly loosen or open. Water knots are notoriously insecure in this way, so they should be carefully inspected before each and every use.

Start the water knot with an overhand in one tail of webbing.

Travelling in the opposite direction, use the other tail to retrace the initial overhand, ensuring that it remains flat and parallel through each turn of the knot.

The resulting water knot should have 2-inch tails.

Conclusion

The knots, hitches, and ropework described in this book represent the selection of the most frequent gestures of the rope to accomplish the most frequent applications in a day of rock climbing. If the reader simply uses the knots and hitches in this book as we have described them, without variation or distortion, hundreds of satisfactory days on the crags can be enjoyed.

However, the point of this book is to elucidate the consideration and analysis that should surround every climber's actions. The rope is simply one of the most consequential opportunities for decision making, irrespective of the popularity of certain usages. The same kind of application heuristic that we use to explore the use of the rope could also be applied to anchoring, selecting and maintaining equipment, creating training regimens, or assessing terrain.

We invite climbers to explore the richness and complexity of the sport by treating all subjects in climbing more fully. There is a tendency in our sport, due to the severity of our environment, to create rigid rules and adhere to them. However, as our culture and our sport have demonstrated, a rigid adherence to prescriptive thinking and protocols can result in an incomplete and often inaccurate understanding of our tools, techniques, and folkcraft.

In the end, our environment has infinite variety. So do we. We are infinitely capable of innovative solutions to problems, and we are infinitely capable of mistakes. Without exception, climbers find themselves in awkward scenarios, and their solutions can salvage a day of climbing or save someone's life. It is impossible to perfectly prepare for every contingency, and therefore a flexible and critical mind is needed to solve problems that range from nuisance to near-miss.

In this text we have striven to impart information, but also to situate the reader to be a critical thinker. In the end we will have offered a satisfactory text if the readers not only are climbing comfortably and securely, but also can COPE with each and every decision they make in the mountains, regardless of whether they perfectly adhere to our applications of the rope.

APPENDIX A

Resources for Practicing Knots and Hitches

Context Game

One of the most common errors in knot tying comes from a slight alteration in the context of the knot tying. Consider the clove hitch, for example. A climber's spatial positioning relative to a rope and a carabiner can have numerous variations. The carabiner can be at eye level, chest level, at the climber's waist, or at the climber's feet. The carabiner can be directly in front of the climber, to her right or her left. The gate of the carabiner can be facing the climber or facing away. The clove hitch can be tied in the air, in one's hands, and then placed into the carabiner. Or, the clove hitch can be built on the carabiner.

The Context Game challenges the climber to practice knots and hitches repetitively, but also in lots of different contexts. Here are a few to master:

Knot or Hitch	Context
Clove hitch	Tie the clove hitch in the air.
Clove hitch	Build the clove hitch on the carabiner.
Munter hitch	Tie the Munter hitch in the air.
Munter hitch	Tie the Munter hitch on the carabiner.

Knot or Hitch	Context
Loaded Munter	If the first application of the Munter is to be loaded, tie the Munter on the carabiner in the load position, instead of flipping it after the fact.
Taking Munter	If the first application of the Munter is to take in slack, tie the Munter on the carabiner in the take position, instead of flipping it after the fact.
Bowline and bowline with a bight	Tie a bowline with the opposite loop; the result will look inverted.
Bowline and bowline with a bight	Tie a bowline around an object, so that the object partially obstructs the view of the knot.
Prusik with a trigger	Tie the Prusik so that the joining knot ends up bridging the friction hitch. This version of the accessory cord loop has a quick-point release, but some tests show it to be a weaker version of the hitch.
Coils with short ropes	Practice all coils with a shorter rope. If the coil is ugly, it will be more obvious.

Online Resources

http://www.animatedknots.com

There are great online resources for practicing knots and hitches. One of the best is Animated Knots by Grog. However, a climber should understand the usefulness of the site. The knots are not tied in context, so the site is a great tool to remember rope mechanics, sequence, and history. It is also a great site for climbers to understand how ropework is a craft that is necessary in lots of outdoor pursuits and sports, not just climbing.

But the lack of context in each animation, can be confusing for climbers. The bowline will not be demonstrated in relation to a tree or other stationary object. The clove hitch will not be demonstrated on a carabiner; the figure 8 follow through will not pass through the hard points of a harness. Instead, the climber will need to infer each of these contexts from the demonstration, and that requires some insight into the sport, the application of the knot, and imagination.

http://www.netknots.com

Net Knots is another informative site and the animations there can be easy to follow. However, much like Animated Knots, the lack of real-world applications and context means that the climber will need a bit of forethought and imagination to gain much value from the site.

Lastly, there are a myriad of videos, blogs, informational websites, and other open-source sites and resources for a savvy user of the Internet to discover. Many of these resources are valuable but many of them are not. It is important to use your judgment and discretion when perusing these tools. Blog posts and YouTube videos are often posted by well-intentioned but witless practitioners, and their absolute conviction about a certain technique, ropework, knot, or hitch can be quite persuasive. In the end, a climber's own judgment and discretion can be enhanced by asking a few simple questions:

- Is the video professionally produced?
- Does the presenter have either credentials in climbing (AMGA certification) or ropework (textile science, mechanical engineering)?

If the answer is no to either of those questions, it might be prudent to cross-reference the presentation with other resources. There will probably be immediate contradictions, conditional circumstances, or other unexplained phenomena.

Books

Ashley Book of Knots
The encyclopedic nature of this massive tome is at once attractive and a bit of overkill for a casual rock climber. Even though the original author passed away shortly after publication, knot enthusiasts and rope-craft specialists have persevered to update the text with information relevant to modern nylon ropes, ongoing research and knowledge that was not available at the time of the original publication, and a few modern applications. It's a great book to have on the shelf to sort out trivia, knot history, and lore and learn a few rope tricks to impress other climbers. However, the reason every knot in that book is not in this book is because every knot is not always as valuable as a hand-ful of universally applicable knots.

On Rope
With a greater emphasis on application and combined rope systems, *On Rope* is the best written resource for rope craft used in vertical environments. The writers set out to create a definitive resource for these techniques, and their diligence is apparent. Again, their book is so vast in its scope, it might not always be the most practi-cal guide, and every technique therein is not always necessary for an enjoyable day of toproping. But it is hard to argue with the authors' recommendation: "Be

progressive. Be precise. Be the technician that is necessary to remain on the safe leading edge of this craft. Never lose the passion for that which you love."

—*Bruce Smith and Allen Padgett*

Climbing Knot Comparison Chart

The following comparison chart reminds readers of the essential criteria of each knot, hitch, and bend in the book and suggests an application. It can be helpful to see the entire list, and comparing and contrasting is a valuable tool. Remember, the strength, visual clarity, efficiency, security, and failure mechanism of any knot or hitch usually suggests the most common applications. That's part of what it means to COPE with the rope.

Knot or Hitch	Notes on Visual Clarity	Strength	Efficiency	Security	Most Common Applications
Attaching the Rope to a Climber					
Figure 8 follow through	Instantly recognizable due to symmetrical appearance when well dressed.	Retains 80-90% of material strength.	Three steps to tie, not too difficult to untie (depending on load).	Two gestures of rope destabilize the knot.	Tying in to end of rope in a team setting.
Double bowline with Yosemite finish	Difficult to inspect unless specifically familiar with the knot.	Retains 80-90% of material strength.	Four steps to tie, easy to untie (even after forceful loading).	Three gestures of the rope destabilize the knot.	Tying to end of rope when frequent and forceful falls are anticipated (sport climbing).

Attaching the Rope to Something (Climbers or Objects)

Figure 8 on a bight	Same as figure 8 follow through.	Same as figure 8 follow through.	Same as figure 8 follow through.	Same as figure 8 follow through.	Use to attach a rope end to a climber (with 2 locking carabiners) or an object (with one locking carabiner).
Overhand on a bight	Initial overhand knot is distinctly doubled.	Some testers have demonstrated slightly less strength than figure 8.	Two steps to tie, not too difficult to untie (depending on load).	One gesture of the rope can destabilize the knot.	Attaching a bight of rope to a carabiner when strength is a priority and the bight is not in proximity to the rope end.
Bowline	Signature tongue points to anticipated load.	Some testers have demonstrated slightly less strength than figure 8.	Three steps to tie, easy to untie (even after forceful loading).	Two gestures of the rope destabilize the knot.	Tying a rope around an object with an unknown circumference.
Bowline with a bight	Signature tongue is doubled.	Same as bowline, but two strands double strength and durability.	Same as bowline.	Same as bowline.	Tying a bight of rope around an object with a difficult to estimate circumference.

Knot or Hitch	Notes on Visual Clarity	Strength	Efficiency	Security	Most Common Applications
Friction Hitches					
Prusik	Six parallel laps with bridge, one connection loop.	Defaults to strength of joining knot.	Can be tedious to dress perfectly.	Holding power can be compromised by poor dressing.	Grabbing a rope when reliable and optimal gripping power are important.
Autoblock	6-8 parallel wraps, two connection loops.	Behaves erratically. sometimes grips tight, sometimes slips at lower loads.	Quick to tie, quick to untie.	Dressing, material, and circumstance affect holding power.	Grabbing a rope when efficiency and nominal gripping power are important.
Kleimheist	Nose is shorter than wraps and points toward the load.	Defaults to strength of joining knot or bar-tack.	Tedious to tie and requires routine inspection.	Holding power can be compromised by poor dressing.	Tying a friction hitch with a sling.

Joining Knots and Bends

Double fisherman's	Signature side-by-side interlocking Xs and 2-inch tails.	Retains 80-90% of material strength.	Tedious to tie and difficult to untie after being loaded.	Two gestures of the rope destabilize the bend.	Joining two rope ends in a permanent way.
Flat overhand	Same appearance as overhand, but loaded on the flat side it splits the knot; 10-12 inch tails.	With some ropes, capsizing is possible at less than 75% of the material strength.	Quick to tie and quick to untie, even after loading.	Catastrophic capsizing is only possible if flat overhand is proximal to rope ends.	Joining two rope ends in a temporary way where strength and security are less important: rappelling.
Water knot	A flat fist of knot with 2-inch tails.	Retains 80-90% of material strength.	Tedious to tie and requires routine inspection.	One gesture of the tails can destabilize the knot.	Joining flat webbing.

Knot or Hitch	Notes on Visual Clarity	Strength	Efficiency	Security	Most Common Applications
Anchoring and Belaying Hitches					
Clove hitch	Biting loop captures load strand and standing end.	Has been demonstrated to slip at less than 75% of material strength.	Quick to tie and untie.	Carabiner use affects security. Use HMS or pear-shaped carabiners.	Attaching a rope to carabiner when adjustability is more important than strength.
Munter hitch	Biting loop captures load strand and brake hand holds standing end.	Relative to the grip strength of the user.	Quick to tie and untie.	Carabiner use affects security. Use HMS or pear-shaped carabiners.	Belaying or a releasable attachment (when combined with a mule knot).
Mule knot (Munter)	Visually confusing.	Defaults to the strength of the overhand knot.	Tricky to tie, but easy to untie.	Two gestures of the rope destabilize the knot.	Closing the Munter hitch to liberate brake hand.
Mule knot (belay device)	Visually confusing.	Defaults to the strength of the overhand knot.	Tricky to tie, but easy to untie.	Two gestures of the rope destabilize the knot.	Closing the belay device to liberate brake hand.

GriGri stopper (overhand on a bight)	Familiar overhand with a bight.	Defaults to strength of the GriGri.	Quick to tie, quick to untie.	One gesture of the rope destabilizes the knot, but it is backing up a stable GriGri.	Closing the GriGri to liberate the brake hand.

Creating a Master Point

BHK	Looks like a big honking knot. Often has signature loop to manage.	Same as an overhand or figure 8 but the BHK is tied in two or more strands of material, increasing the strength.	Quick to tie, quick to untie	Knot cannot be destabilized when in use.	Constructing a materially redundant master point.

Knot or Hitch	Notes on Visual Clarity	Strength	Efficiency	Security	Most Common Applications
Rope Coils					
New England coil	Wraps in middle create two equally sized groups of rope loops.	N/A	Coiling a single strand takes longer, but it's easy to flake out.	N/A	Transporting a rope on or across a backpack.
Double butterfly coil	Long tails coming out of the head of the coil can be used as backpack straps.	N/A	Coiling a double strand is fast, but causes problems when flaking out the coil.	N/A	Coiling rapidly for quick transport or short carries.
Mountaineer's coil	Concentric loops create the iconic coil.	N/A	Coiling and flaking out is tedious.	N/A	Comfortable to carry without a backpack and cool looking.

APPENDIX C

Knots Conspicuously Missing from This Book

We are routinely asked about certain knots and hitches that are conspicuously missing from our courses, and they are also missing from this book. Some climbers will discover pet applications of these knots, but they have not proven themselves to be the most useful in a career of rock climbing.

Bachmann's Hitch

While the Bachmann's is a favorite hitch for those climbers who routinely travel on fixed ropes, it does not excel in that task in any particular way. Its fans love the way the carabiner inside the wraps of the friction hitch create an easy-to-find release for sliding the friction hitch along a rope. That carabiner can only be moved in one direction, however, and it is easy to destabilize the hitch simply by grabbing the enwrapped carabiner. In total, the Bachmann's wins a place in many climbers' hearts, but it is a hitch than can easily be done without. It neither grabs more

The Bachmann's has its signature point release in the wrapped carabiner handle but doesn't prove more effective in any application than a Prusik or an autoblock.

tightly than a Prusik, nor does it deploy more efficiently than an autoblock.

Double Overhand or Stopper Knot

The double overhand or stopper knot is a favorite for closing the system when lowering, rappelling, and belaying. But its proximity to the rope end can make it susceptible to capsizing, and a single gesture of the rope end destabilizes the knot. There is a reason

The stopper knot is commonly used to closed a rappel or belay system.

why rope manufacturers, like Petzl, recommend the overhand on a bight for these applications: It's more familiar, more secure, and provides a nice flat edge to ram into a belay or rappel system. Nevertheless, the stopper knot is a favorite for many climbers.

Bunny Eared Eight and the Bowline on a Bight

The bunny eared eight and the bowline on a bight are commonly mistaken for materially redundant knot configurations, like the BHK. However, they both default to a single point of failure, a single strand that girth hitches the entire knot. If this single strand were to be compromised, all the loops in the knot would be compromised too. Many climbers learn to rely on these two knots to affix a rope to a pair of strong components, like bolts. In this application and others, redundancy is not even a goal, so the nonredundant makes sense. Futhermore, that single strand that girth

The bunny eared eight is not a redundant knot, but it can be used to connect a rope to two separate carabiners.

hitches the knot can be adjusted to offset the size of the two attachment loops. Many climbers love the way these kinds of adjustments allow them to distribute load to components when the fall line of the fixed line tends to be widely variable. But these applications are more rare, and so the knots become very specialized in their application. Climbing instructors use these knots quite regularly, but they are not always that useful for a day of toproping.

Like the bunny eared eight, the bowline on a bight can be used to offset two attachment loops and is easily adjusted in the process. Perfect for attaching a fixed line to two components.

Traditional Mule Knot on a Plate/ Aperture/Tuber Belay Device

Traditionally the mule knot has been tied in this configuration and backed up with an overhand on a bight. This method avoids using the spine of the attachment carabiner. Some find the traditional method cumbersome to tie, difficult to reduce in a precise manner, or difficult to maintain the brake strand/avoid slippage. An HMS or pear-shaped locking carabiner, while still recommended, is not required for this application. This may be the best indication of when to use this version.

Traditionally the mule knot has been tied such that all the tying is done above the belay device after an initial pass back through the carabiner.

About the Authors

Nate Fitch is a faculty member in the renowned Outdoor Education Department at the University of New Hampshire specializing in climbing courses/programming, and is the director of the Gass Climbing Center. He is an AMGA-Certified Single Pitch Instructor and apprentice rock guide who is also active in providing AMGA instructor programs in the climbing wall and single pitch disciplines. He lives with his wife and two kids in Durham, New Hampshire.

Ron Funderburke is an AMGA-Certified Rock Guide. He is also a senior guide with Fox Mountain Guides and an AMGA SPI discipline coordinator.

FIND A GUIDE » BECOME ONE

AMERICAN MOUNTAIN GUIDES ASSOCIATION

1979

AMGA.COM

PROTECTING CLIMBING **ACCESS** SINCE 199'

| JOIN US |
WWW.ACCESSFUND.ORG